SPARKS OF LIFE

Chemical Elements that Make Life Possible

OXYGEN

by

Jean F. Blashfield

RSVP®
RAINTREE
STECK-VAUGHN
PUBLISHERS
A Steck-Vaughn Company

Austin, Texas

Special thanks to our technical consultant,
Jeanne Hamers, Ph.D.,
formerly with the Institute of Chemical Education,
Madison, Wisconsin

Development: Books Two, Delavan, Wisconsin
Graphics: Krueger Graphics, Janesville, Wisconsin
Interior Design: Peg Esposito
Photo Research and Indexing: Margie Benson

Raintree Steck-Vaughn Publisher's Staff:
Publishing Director: Walter Kossmann   Project Editor: Frank Tarsitano
Design Manager: Joyce Spicer   Electronic Production: Scott Melcer

Library of Congress Cataloging-in-Publication Data:
Blashfield, Jean F.
        Oxygen / by Jean F. Blashfield.
             p.   cm. — (Sparks of life)
        Includes bibliographical references (p.   -   ) and index.
        Summary: Presents the basic concepts of oxygen, the most important chemical element in our lives and also the most abundant element in nature.
        ISBN 0-8172-5037-9
        1. Oxygen — Juvenile literature. [1. Oxygen.] I. Title. II. Series: Blashfield, Jean F.   Sparks of life.
        QD181.01B53   1999   98-4508
        546' .721 — dc21   CIP   AC

Printed and bound in the United States
 2 3 4 5 6 7 8 9 LB 03 02 01 00 99

PHOTO CREDITS: Photo Courtesy of the American Council on Exercise, Copyright 1997 26; © Archive Photos 9, 13, 54; Aurora Health Care 46; BASF 45; Bethlehem Steel cover, 41; © B.I.F.C., cover, 22; Corbis-Bettman 11; © Liane Enkelis, Stock Boston 43; © Beverly Factor, International Stock cover; Photo by Charles Jagoe, USF&WS 30 inset; ©1997 Steven Holt/Aigrette cover; JLM Visuals 25, 32 top, 35; Dennis Kunkel, University of Hawaii, Used with Permission 29; Medichrome/Div. The Stock Shop Inc. cover; Milwaukee Public Museum 51; NASA 21, 40, 57; United Water 36; USDA–ARS Information Staff 8; U.S. Navy Photo 30; Wisconsin Department of Natural Resources 49; Woods Hole Oceanographic Institution 34.

CONTENTS

Periodic Table of the Elements

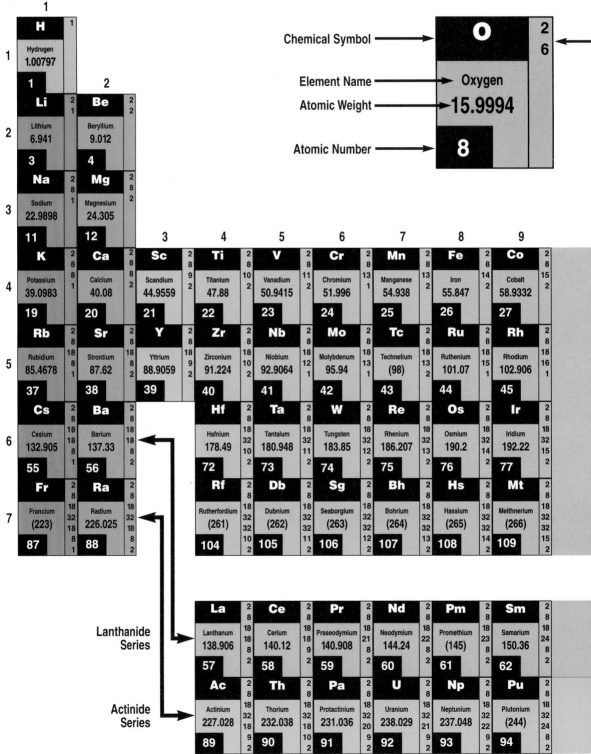

Number of electrons in each shell,
beginning with the K shell, top.

See next page for explanations.

							18
							He 2
							Helium
							4.0026
				13	14	15	16	17	2

13	14	15	16	17	
B 2 3	**C** 2 4	**N** 2 5	**O** 2 6	**F** 2 7	**Ne** 2 8
Boron 10.81	Carbon 12.011	Nitrogen 14.0067	Oxygen 15.9994	Fluorine 18.9984	Neon 20.179
5	6	7	8	9	10
Al 2 8 3	**Si** 2 8 4	**P** 2 8 5	**S** 2 8 6	**Cl** 2 8 7	**Ar** 2 8 8
Aluminum 26.9815	Silicon 28.0855	Phosphorus 30.9738	Sulfur 32.06	Chlorine 35.453	Argon 39.948
13	14	15	16	17	18

10	11	12	13	14	15	16	17	18
Ni 2 8 16 2	**Cu** 2 8 18 1	**Zn** 2 8 18 2	**Ga** 2 8 18 3	**Ge** 2 8 18 4	**As** 2 8 18 5	**Se** 2 8 18 6	**Br** 2 8 18 7	**Kr** 2 8 18 8
Nickel 58.69	Copper 63.546	Zinc 65.39	Gallium 69.72	Germanium 72.59	Arsenic 74.9216	Selenium 78.96	Bromine 79.904	Krypton 83.80
28	29	30	31	32	33	34	35	36
Pd 2 8 18 18	**Ag** 2 8 18 18 1	**Cd** 2 8 18 18 2	**In** 2 8 18 18 3	**Sn** 2 8 18 18 4	**Sb** 2 8 18 18 5	**Te** 2 8 18 18 6	**I** 2 8 18 18 7	**Xe** 2 8 18 18 8
Palladium 106.42	Silver 107.868	Cadmium 112.41	Indium 114.82	Tin 118.71	Antimony 121.75	Tellurium 127.6	Iodine 126.905	Xenon 131.29
46	47	48	49	50	51	52	53	54
Pt 2 8 18 32 17	**Au** 2 8 18 32 1	**Hg** 2 8 18 32 18 1	**Tl** 2 8 18 32 18 3	**Pb** 2 8 18 32 18 4	**Bi** 2 8 18 32 18 5	**Po** 2 8 18 32 18 6	**At** 2 8 18 32 18 7	**Rn** 2 8 18 32 18 8
Platinum 195.08	Gold 196.967	Mercury 200.59	Thallium 204.383	Lead 207.2	Bismuth 208.98	Polonium (209)	Astatine (210)	Radon (222)
78	79	80	81	82	83	84	85	86
(Uun) 2 8 18 32 32 17 1	**(Unu)** 2 8 18 32 32 18 1	**(Uub)** 2 8 18 32 32 18 2						
(Ununnilium) (269)	(Unununium) (272)	(Ununbium) (277)						
110	111	112						

Alkali Metals	Transition Metals	Nonmetals	Metalloids	Lanthanide Series
Alkaline Earth Metals	Other Metals	Noble Gases	Actinide Series	COLOR KEYS

Eu 2 8 18 25 8 2	**Gd** 2 8 18 25 9 2	**Tb** 2 8 18 27 8 2	**Dy** 2 8 18 28 8 2	**Ho** 2 8 18 29 8 2	**Er** 2 8 18 30 8 2	**Tm** 2 8 18 31 8 2	**Yb** 2 8 18 32 8 2	**Lu** 2 8 18 32 9 2
Europium 151.96	Gadolinium 157.25	Terbium 158.925	Dysprosium 162.50	Holmium 164.93	Erbium 167.26	Thulium 168.934	Ytterbium 173.04	Lutetium 174.967
63	64	65	66	67	68	69	70	71
Am 2 8 18 32 25 8 2	**Cm** 2 8 18 32 25 9 2	**Bk** 2 8 18 32 26 9 2	**Cf** 2 8 18 32 28 8 2	**Es** 2 8 18 32 29 8 2	**Fm** 2 8 18 32 30 8 2	**Md** 2 8 18 32 31 8 2	**No** 2 8 18 32 32 8 2	**Lr** 2 8 18 32 32 9 2
Americium (243)	Curium (247)	Berkelium (247)	Californium (251)	Einsteinium (254)	Fermium (257)	Mendelevium (258)	Nobelium (259)	Lawrencium (260)
95	96	97	98	99	100	101	102	103

A Guide to the Periodic Table

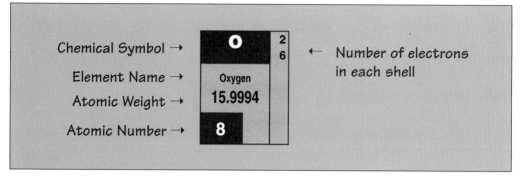

Symbol = an abbreviation of an element name, agreed on by members of the International Union of Pure and Applied Chemistry. The idea to use symbols was started by a Swedish chemist, Jöns Jakob Berzelius, about 1814. Note that the elements with numbers 110, 111, and 112, which were "discovered" in 1996, have not yet been given official names.

Atomic number = the number of protons (particles with a positive charge) in the nucleus of an atom of an element; also equal to the number of electrons (particles with a negative charge) found in the shells, or rings, of an atom that does not have an electrical charge.

Atomic weight = the weight of an element compared to a standard element, carbon. When the Periodic Table was first developed, hydrogen was used as the standard. It was given an atomic weight of 1, but that created some difficulties, and in 1962, the standard was changed to carbon-12, which is the most common form of the element carbon, with an atomic weight of 12.

The Periodic Table on pages 4 and 5 shows the atomic weight of carbon as 12.011 because an atomic weight is an average of the weights, or masses, of all the different naturally occurring forms of an atom. Each form, called an isotope, has a different number of neutrons (uncharged particles) in the nucleus. Most elements have several isotopes, but chemists assume that any two samples of an element are made up of the same mixture of isotopes and thus have the same mass, or weight.

Electron shells = regions surrounding the nucleus of an atom in which the electrons move. Historically, electron shells have been described as orbits similar to a planet's orbit. But actually they are whole areas of a specific energy level, in which certain electrons vibrate and move around. The shell closest to the nucleus, the K shell, can contain only 2 electrons. The K shell has the lowest energy level, and it is very hard to break its electrons away. The second shell, L, can contain only 8 electrons. Others may contain up to 32 electrons. The outer shell; in which chemical reactions occur, is called the valence shell.

Periods = horizontal rows of elements in the Periodic Table. A period contains all the elements with the same number of orbital shells of electrons. Note that the actinide and lanthanide (or rare earth) elements shown in rows below the main table really belong within the table, but it is not regarded as practical to print such a wide table as would be required.

Groups = vertical columns of elements in the Periodic Table; also called families. A group contains all elements that naturally have the same number of electrons in the outermost shell or orbital of the atom. Elements in a group tend to behave in similar ways.

Group 1 = alkali metals: very reactive and never found in nature in their pure form. Bright, soft metals, they have one valence electron and, like all metals, conduct both electricity and heat.

Group 2 = alkaline earth metals: also very reactive and thus do not occur in pure form in nature. Harder and denser than alkali metals, they have two valence electrons that easily combine with other chemicals.

Groups 3–12 = transition metals: the great mass of metals, with a variable number of electrons; can exist in pure form.

Groups 13–17 = metals, metalloids, and nonmetals. Metalloids possess some characteristics of metals and some of nonmetals. Unlike metals and metalloids, nonmetals do not conduct electricity.

Group 18 = noble, or rare, gases. In general, these nonmetallic gaseous elements do not react with other elements because their valence shells are full.

THE SEARCH FOR THE INVISIBLE

The chemical element called oxygen is an invisible gas in the air we breathe. In fact, we must breathe oxygen to live. But oxygen is also in the rocks beneath our feet and in the water we drink.

Oxygen is one of the most important chemical elements in our lives. Fortunately, oxygen is also the most abundant element in the earth's crust.

But we don't usually see oxygen, smell it, or taste it. Early scientists did not even suspect it was part of our air.

Throughout most of history, people believed that there were just four elements, or basic substances that could not be broken down—earth, air, fire, and water. From the time of the ancient Greeks, people believed that everything else in the universe was made up of these four elements. Oddly enough, we now know that there is one element important to all four, and that element is oxygen.

About A.D. 800, a Chinese writer suggested that air was not an element but a mixture of two gases, which he called "complete air" and "incomplete air." The "complete air" is now thought to have been nitrogen (N, element #7), while the incomplete air was oxygen. European scientists had no access to the writings of the Chinese, and they could not build on this suggestion.

In the fifteenth century, Italian scientist and artist Leonardo da Vinci also suggested that air was a mixture of at least two gases. He recognized that something in air was required by animals to live, but he didn't investigate that idea.

Early science often involved superstition and magic. The people who tried to make magical changes in the common substances around them were called alchemists. Alchemy (a term that may originally have meant "the Egyptian art") was a mixture of science, magic, religion, and hope.

An alchemist at work in his laboratory, mixing chemistry, religion, and perhaps some magic to understand the physical world

One thing alchemists hoped to discover was what makes things burn. Fire seemed magical, and they thought that if they understood fire, they might understand everything.

The search gradually became important for more practical reasons. People were beginning to discover the possibilities of steam power, and it seemed important to understand how fire, which turns water into useful steam, worked.

German alchemist Johann Becher proposed about 1680 that some matter contains a flammable (burnable) substance, to which he gave the Latin name *terra pinguis,* meaning "fatty earth." When the matter is burned, the *terra pinguis* is given off.

German alchemist (or perhaps he was now a chemist) Georg Ernst Stahl, a pupil of Becher's, called the invisible substance that makes fire burn phlogiston, which means "able to be burned." He thought that air had nothing to do with burning. It just served as a means of transporting phlogiston out of a burning material and moving it to something else. Stahl also recognized that the process of iron (Fe, element #26) rusting was somewhat like fire burning. He thought that as iron rusted, it also gave off phlogiston but more slowly than when something was burned.

For the next hundred years, chemists accepted the phlogiston theory and ignored anything they observed that didn't seem to fit into the theory. One unfortunate habit left over from alchemy was the belief that it was not necessary to weigh the materials being studied. These early chemists assumed that it would be no more possible to collect a bottle of phlogiston than it would be to collect a bottle of magnetism. Phlogiston was just a quality of matter.

Those who did measure the components of an experiment, however, discovered that some substances when heated actually gained weight instead of losing weight. That finding was in opposition to the phlogiston theory. The staunch believers in the theory ignored that discovery.

Swedish chemist Carl Wilhelm Scheele (at the desk), working with an assistant. Scheele discovered many elements.

The Unlucky Swede

Carl Wilhelm Scheele of Sweden was an apothecary, or pharmacist, in the 1700s. Unlike most of today's pharmacists, he manufactured his own medicines and was actually a chemist. Scheele was different from most chemists of his time in that he measured the materials he worked with. He investigated just about every problem that came his way, discovering numerous acids, exploring poisons, and even discovering a chemical principal that was later used in photography.

Scheele played a role in the discovery of many elements, including manganese (Mn, element #25), molybdenum (Mo, #42), and chlorine (Cl, #17), but he received credit for little of his work. Even the discovery of oxygen, which Scheele accomplished first, has often been credited to Englishman Joseph Priestley. Priestley hurried to publish his observations, while Scheele tended to be slow in writing up his work and getting it published.

Scheele proposed that air was made up of two main gases. Working with a variety of chemicals about 1770, he was able to separate out one gas, which he called "fire air" because things burned in it. This was the first known separation and collection of oxygen. However, the apothecary stuck to the idea of phlogiston and did not really understand what his "fire air" was.

Scheele called the second gas in air "spoiled air" because it didn't support life. The major part of that "spoiled air" would later be identified by Scottish scientist Daniel Rutherford as nitrogen, the Chinese writer's "complete air."

In the end, it was probably Scheele's scientific curiosity that killed him. He had a very dangerous habit of tasting many of the compounds he created. Although no one specific experiment killed him, he died at the age of forty-three with symptoms that sound like poisoning by mercury (Hg, element #80).

The Curious Englishman

Joseph Priestley was an English clergyman and teacher who relished experimenting with electricity, chemicals, and whatever else caught his attention. His research was just a hobby until 1766 when he met a visiting American, Benjamin Franklin, in London. Priestley was fascinated by the American political leader's scientific studies, and Priestley, too, began to devote himself to science. In the 1770s, Priestley worked as a librarian and companion to Lord Shelburne, in order to have time to carry out studies into the various known gases, including air.

Priestley discovered that if he heated the element mercury,

Joseph Priestley

which is a silver liquid, in air, the mercury changed into a dark orange-colored powder, later identified as mercuric oxide. He was using a magnifying lens to study some of the powder in a test tube one day in 1774 when the sun's rays, concentrated by the lens, heated the powder. Mysteriously, the orange powder changed back into droplets of silver liquid.

This clergyman who had already studied many gases discovered that as the mercuric oxide changed back into silver droplets, it gave off a gas. He captured some of the gas and found that things placed in the gas burned even better than they did in air. Priestley, also unwilling to give up the idea of phlogiston, called the gas "dephlogisticated air."

Going to Paris, Priestley introduced himself to chemist Antoine Lavoisier and told him of his work. At that point, the story of the discovery of oxygen became Lavoisier's story.

Priestley himself became an enthusiastic Unitarian as well as a supporter of France and the French Revolution. These enthusiasms angered his neighbors, and eventually he was forced to leave England. Priestley moved to the United States where he lived in Pennsylvania—the state of his old friend, Ben Franklin—until his death in 1804.

Lavoisier, the Revolutionary

At a time when revolutionary politics was common, French chemist Antoine Laurent Lavoisier was a revolutionary in the field of science, not politics. But the supporters of the French Revolution eventually killed him anyway.

No one took a really clear look at the phlogiston theory until Lavoisier came on the scene about 1770. He was unwilling to ignore facts that didn't fit the theory. He acquired information from everywhere and then tested it for himself, making him the first chemist to use the modern scientific method. Most importantly, he measured and recorded every step of every procedure.

However, Lavoisier was not always ethical about giving credit where it was due when he repeated experiments first performed by other people. He barely acknowledged that Priestley had anything to do with discovering oxygen, and he tried for years to take credit for Henry Cavendish's discovery of the elements that make water. However, Lavoisier managed to get rid of most of the old, useless ideas of alchemy and put chemistry on a firm, modern footing.

Lavoisier gave the name *oxygène* to Priestley's "dephlogisticated air." The name means "acid-forming," though Lavoisier was wrong in thinking that all acids must contain oxygen.

Lavoisier determined that oxygen was the important element in both combustion (fire) and in respiration (breathing). And he realized that both these processes combine oxygen with other elements, making them gain weight. And so the long-lived phlogiston theory was finally thrown out.

As a footnote, Lavoisier was part owner of a company that collected taxes for the government by unfair means. After the French Revolution began and revolutionaries gained control of the French government, the tax collectors, including Lavoisier, were arrested and beheaded.

A French mathematician, Joseph Louis Lagrange, acknowledged science's debt to the arrogant Lavoisier when he wrote: "It took but a moment to cut off that head; perhaps a hundred years will be required to produce another like it."

BUSY
OXYGEN
ATOMS

Oxygen is element number 8 (atomic number 8), because it has eight protons (positively charged particles) in its central nucleus. Most oxygen atoms also have eight neutrons (particles with no electrical charge) in the nucleus.

An oxygen atom has eight electrons (negatively charged particles) in continuous motion around the nucleus. Two electrons move within the first region, or shell, closest to the nucleus. The second, or outer shell, has only six electrons instead of the eight electrons that a filled second shell would have. A filled outer shell is more stable than one with "holes" in it and, therefore, less likely to react with other atoms.

Chemical reactions happen because atoms of the same or different elements join so that their outer electron shells become complete. This state can be achieved by atoms sharing electrons or

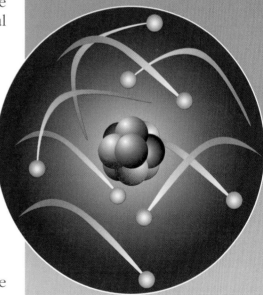

by one atom gaining and another atom losing electrons in the outer shell. Because oxygen has only six electrons in its outer shell, it has an "urge" to link up with other elements that will provide electrons to complete that outer shell. Oxygen is located in Group 16 of the Periodic Table (see pages 4 and 5). All the elements in that group have only six electrons, called valence electrons, in their outer shells. The elements in Group 16 include sulfur (S, element #16), selenium (Se, #34), tellurium (Te, #52), and polonium (Po, #84).

Because of its urge to react (its instability), pure oxygen gas is not a collection of single atoms. It occurs as a diatomic (or

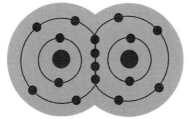

Two oxygen atoms bond together to make a diatomic molecule by sharing two pairs of electrons, which completes each atom's outer, or valence, shell.

two-atomed) element. That means that most oxygen molecules consist of two atoms of oxygen linked together by sharing electrons so that each one has a filled outer shell. Diatomic oxygen, or O_2, molecules are stable. Other diatomic elements include hydrogen (H, element #1), chlorine, and nitrogen.

Sometimes the energy of sunlight hitting O_2 molecules in the atmosphere breaks them apart. That leaves single O atoms adrift. Again, such atoms are very unstable, so they quickly attach themselves to O_2 molecules, making another form of oxygen, O_3, which is better known as ozone. Oxygen molecules must have energy added before they start forming ozone molecules. Electricity provides this energy, which is why the slight "burning" smell of ozone occurs after a lightning strike, and sometimes near electrical equipment. Ozone is a pale-blue gas.

Loose oxygen atoms may also attract single atoms from ozone molecules, thus producing more stable O_2 molecules. This series of reactions is continually going on in the atmosphere:

$$O + O \rightarrow O_2$$

$$3O_2 + energy \rightarrow 2O_3$$

$$O_3 + O + sunlight \rightarrow 2O_2$$

Of course, oxygen atoms don't react only with themselves. In fact, oxygen is one of the most reactive elements there is. The addition of oxygen to an atom or molecule can change the characteristics of the element or compound very much. Dihydrogen oxide, H_2O, is better known as water. But if one more atom of oxygen is added to the molecule, it becomes hydrogen peroxide, H_2O_2. ("Per" at the beginning of a chemical name means that it has two or more oxygen atoms.) The discoverer of hydrogen peroxide, French scientist Louis Jacques Thénard, called it "oxygenated water." If you have had your ears pierced, you may have used hydrogen peroxide as a disinfectant to keep the holes from becoming infected.

Oxidation

Oxygen readily combines with many elements by accepting electrons to fill its outer valence shell. An element that combines with oxygen in this manner is said to have been oxidized. Because oxidation is such a common reaction, the term is used for the process of any element gaining electrons, even if the process does not involve oxygen.

Similarly, an element that gives up electrons in making a molecule is said to be involved in a reduction process. You can't have one without the other, so the total process is called a reduction-oxidation process, or redox. The most common redox reaction is combustion. Also, when oxygen combines with molecules in the body in a redox reaction, energy is given off.

Isotopes

The most common form of oxygen has a total of 16 particles—8 protons and 8 neutrons—in its nucleus. This common oxygen is called oxygen-16. Other naturally occurring forms, or isotopes, are O-17 and O-18. (The word *isotope* means "same place," because all isotopes of an element occupy the same place in the Periodic Table.) They are mixed in with O-16 at all times, but we don't notice them in the air. The oxygen in the air we breathe contains 99.76 percent O-16. The remaining 0.24 percent consists of varying amounts of O-17 and O-18.

Other isotopes of oxygen—12, 13, 14, 15, and 19 through 24—are radioactive and very short-lived. They may result from natural decay processes or by processes initiated by scientists.

If only O-16 existed, oxygen's atomic weight (or mass number) would be 16. But the small amounts of other isotopes are averaged in to the mass weight in the same proportions as the isotopes exist in nature. This calculation gives oxygen as a whole an atomic weight of 15.9994.

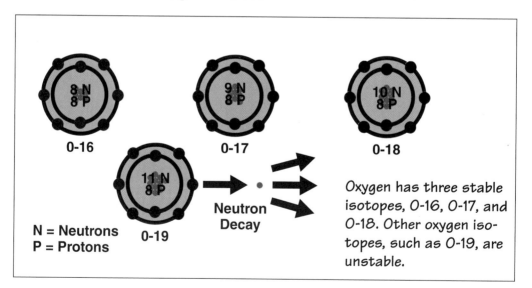

8 N
8 P

0-16

9 N
8 P

0-17

10 N
8 P

0-18

11 N
8 P

0-19

Neutron
Decay

N = Neutrons
P = Protons

Oxygen has three stable isotopes, O-16, O-17, and O-18. Other oxygen isotopes, such as O-19, are unstable.

OXYGEN IN OUR WORLD

Oxygen is one of the most important elements in our world, yet it makes up less than 1 percent of the universe. Much more abundant are hydrogen—76 percent—and helium (He, element #2)—23 percent. Everything else in the entire universe, including oxygen, fits into the 1 percent left over.

Scientists of old could not really understand what they called the four elements—air, fire, water, and earth—until oxygen was discovered. Then they found that this true element is part of all four.

Oxygen in the Air

Oxygen makes up about one-fifth (20.95 percent) of Earth's atmosphere. It has been estimated that our atmosphere contains about 1,160,000,000,000,000 (that's 1,160 trillion!) tons of oxygen. The oxygen is not combined chemically with the other elements that make up air. Instead, air is a mixture—the individual gases do not combine. The oxygen is

Universe: less than 1% oxygen

Atmosphere: 20.95%

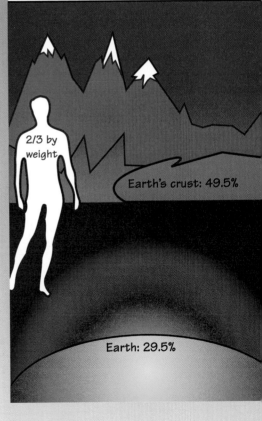

2/3 by weight

Earth's crust: 49.5%

Earth: 29.5%

19

Others less than 0.002%

Carbon dioxide 0.035%

Argon 0.94%

Oxygen
20.9 %

Nitrogen
78.08 %

COMPONENTS OF DRY AIR

available for animals and plants to breathe and for other elements to react with.

In addition to the individual gaseous atoms and molecules shown at the left, several other gaseous compounds add to the total of combined oxygen in the air. These include several different oxides of nitrogen, carbon monoxide (CO), sulfur dioxide (SO_2), and ozone (O_3). (Carbon is C, element #6.) The percentages of these impurities vary with the location at which the measurements are taken.

Earth did not always have an oxidizing atmosphere. In Earth's early history—before life got its start—the atmosphere probably contained no more than 0.002 percent oxygen. Then, in the primeval waters of the planet, primitive plants called blue-green algae began to develop. They were able to utilize the small amount of carbon dioxide present. As a result of making their own food from that carbon dioxide—in a process called photosynthesis—they gave off oxygen. As plants evolved and spread, so did their waste product, oxygen. Gradually, Earth's atmosphere changed into an oxidizing atmosphere. The materials of Earth's crust were gradually oxidized. Most of our mineral resources occur as oxides.

A common reaction is the oxidation of iron into iron oxide, which is officially called ferric oxide (Fe_2O_3) because Fe, the symbol for iron is short for the Latin name, *ferrum*.

You know iron oxide better as rust. It's the reddish, powdery crust that forms on iron products exposed to air. If left for a long time, eventually the iron oxidizes completely and the product disintegrates. A car that develops a rust spot where paint has chipped off should have the spot treated to protect it from further oxidation. Otherwise a hole will develop.

Oxygen in the Solar System

The only other planets known for sure to have oxygen in their atmospheres are Venus and Mars. However, that oxygen is not free. It is bound up with the element carbon as carbon dioxide, CO_2. The oxygen in Mars's atmosphere has changed the iron in the planet's rocks into iron oxide, turning the planet's color to rusty red.

In 1996, observations made with the Hubble Space Telescope revealed that there is probably a very thin atmosphere of oxygen around Jupiter's fourth largest moon, Europa. Molecules in an atmosphere are continually on the move, and scientists define an atmosphere as a gaseous mixture that is dense enough for the

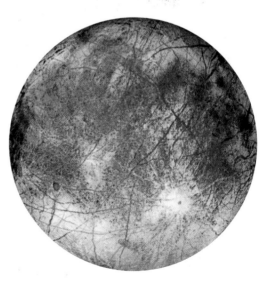

Europa is Jupiter's Earth-like satellite, shown here in a photograph taken by the Galileo spacecraft. The white areas are probably water ice, the brown areas are rock, and the long, dark straight lines are fracture lines on the surface.

molecules to strike one another before escaping into space. Apparently, Europa's oxygen molecules hit three or four others before escaping.

Because the satellite—which is the size of Earth's moon—has virtually no gravity, that thin atmosphere must be generated somehow. Scientists conjecture that there must be water on Europa. Charged particles in Jupiter's magnetic field may knock water molecules free and break some into O_2 and H_2, forming an atmosphere. The O_2 collides with the charged particles making a glow too faint to be seen except by the Space Telescope.

Oxygen in Fire

The "element" that so intrigued alchemists—fire—is not an element at all. It is the heat and light given off during a rapid oxidation process. Rust is slow oxidation, while fire is very quick oxidation, also called combustion.

Most things that burn contain some of the element carbon. Wood is mostly carbon. In the process of burning

A fire will continue to burn as long as it receives oxygen and has fresh material to feed it. Forest-fire fighters try to limit the supply of both factors in order to control a fire.

(or oxidizing), the carbon combines with oxygen, producing carbon dioxide and heat:

$$C + O_2 \rightarrow CO_2 + heat$$

Once a fire has been started, it easily keeps going because the warmer the materials become, the more reactive they are. The addition of more oxygen to a fire makes the fire burn hotter. People who have fireplaces at home often use bellows to pump additional air into a fire, encouraging it to burn hotter.

Slow oxidation can lead to combustion in the dangerous process called spontaneous combustion. Flammable materials—such as rags used in wiping oily car engines, or coal piles, or a haystack—oxidize slowly. But if the heat given off by the oxidation can't dissipate because the materials are in an enclosed space, they may reach a high enough temperature to combust. The result can be a serious fire. A situation that might encourage spontaneous combustion is one of the things looked for during a fire inspection.

Oddly enough, though fire can't happen without oxygen, and oxygen is used in the process of combustion, oxygen itself does not burn. If you thrust a burning match into a bottle of pure oxygen, it will burn only as long as the match itself has material to burn. Then it will go out.

Oxygen in Water

In oceans, lakes, and rivers, two gases—oxygen and hydrogen—are combined to form a liquid oxide. The oxide of hydrogen is, of course, water. But that oxygen is not available for animals to breathe. It's chemically bound to hydrogen. The oxygen used by animals in water is not actually part of the water. It is dissolved in the water and remains chemically free to be used by living things.

Water samples taken from various places often seem to be

different in taste and smell. But it is the other things added to the water that make those differences. Water itself is the same everywhere. It is a chemical compound made up by weight of 11.2 percent hydrogen and 88.8 percent oxygen. A water molecule consists of two hydrogen atoms bound to one oxygen atom:

$$2H_2 + O_2 \rightarrow 2H_2O$$

If you heat water until it boils and keep it boiling, it gradually disappears. It goes into the air as invisible water vapor. When you see steam, you're actually seeing water droplets, not water vapor. The vapor is invisible, but it's still water. It takes the application of electricity to water, in a process called electrolysis, to break water back into its elements.

The hotter water gets, the less dissolved oxygen it can hold. So when water has been boiled, it tastes funny, often described as "flat." It no longer has oxygen dissolved in it. Sometimes a storm or an accident pollutes a city's water system, and the residents are asked to boil their water for safety's sake until the problem is fixed. After being boiled, the water doesn't taste good unless air is stirred into it again.

Oxygen in the Earth

Oxygen makes up 49.5 percent of our planet's crust. The oxygen in rocks is the same oxygen that is invisible in air, but in rocks it is chemically combined with other elements. In fact, the ten most common minerals making up our Earth are oxides.

Silicon (Si, element #14) and oxygen are the most abundant elements in Earth's crust. Most rocks contain minerals consisting of silicon and oxygen, SiO_2, called silicates. The sands of the seas and the beaches are made of broken-up silicates, but so too are many semiprecious stones. Purple-colored amethyst, for example, is quartz, one of the most common silicates, with iron and manganese added.

Oxides of other elements are also found in rocks. The mineral ore called bauxite is an oxide of aluminum (Al, element #13), hematite is an oxide of iron, and magnetite is an oxide of magnesium (Mg, element #12). Many such metals can be extracted from their oxide ores just by removing the oxygen, though the process is not as easy as it sounds. Actually, there's a lot more oxygen combined in the rocks of Earth than there is in all living things and the atmosphere combined. One scientist estimated that there is at least fifty times more oxygen bound up in rocks than in the seas or air.

TOP TEN MINERAL OXIDES

Silicon dioxide, SiO_2 (43% of total oxides) - sand, feldspar
Magnesium oxide, MgO (35%) - magnetite, dolomite
Ferrous oxide, FeO (9%) - hematite
Aluminum oxide, Al_2O_3 (7%) - bauxite
Calcium oxide, CaO (4.4%) - limestone
Sodium oxide, Na_2O (0.45%) - saltpeter
Ferric oxide, Fe_2O_3 (0.36%) - hematite
Titanium dioxide, TiO_2 (0.33%) - titanium ore
Chromic oxide, Cr_2O_3 (0.18%) - chromite
Manganese oxide, MnO (0.14%) - pyrolucite

Amethyst (right) is a semiprecious purple variety of silicon dioxide.

THE BREATH OF LIFE

An exercise physiologist measures a rider's oxygen use during exercise on a special bicycle.

The oxygen content of the human body is mostly bound up as part of water, which makes up about 70 percent of the body. The brain is about 85 percent water. Even the skin, which seems made to keep water out, is about 70 percent water. Bone, of course, contains a lot less. We can go without fresh supplies of water for several days, but we cannot live without oxygen for more than just a few minutes.

Almost all living things take in oxygen, use it in some way, and give off a new chemical, carbon dioxide (CO_2). This process is called respiration. In respiration, oxygen is taken into the living body where it "burns," or breaks down, sugars, releasing the energy in them. As a result of this "burning," the plant or animal has energy to grow, repair its cells, reproduce, and carry on living. Carbon dioxide forms and is given off.

Most animals take in oxygen through

their lungs or other breathing organs. The oxygen gets into the cells, where it oxidizes, or burns, food, giving off heat and energy in the process. Of course, bits of food don't actually get into the cell. The digestive process changes our food into glucose, a sugar, which can enter cells. In the cell, glucose reacts with oxygen to form water, carbon dioxide, and energy. The carbon dioxide is carried back to the lungs where it is exhaled while fresh oxygen is inhaled during breathing. The water not used by cells and organs accumulates and is eventually given off as urine and perspiration. And the energy, of course, keeps us warm, growing, and going.

How our Lungs Use Oxygen

When we inhale air into our lungs, it goes through a series of smaller and smaller tubes called bronchioles until it reaches very tiny sacs called alveoli. Each little sac is surrounded by a

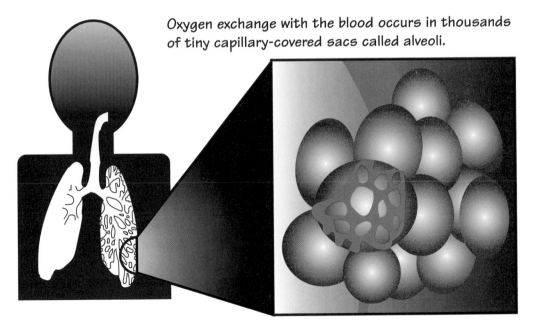

Oxygen exchange with the blood occurs in thousands of tiny capillary-covered sacs called alveoli.

network of capillaries, the tiniest parts of the body's circulatory, or blood, system. When inhaled air reaches the alveoli, only the oxygen separates from the air and passes through the sac membrane into the capillaries. There the red blood cells take it up and carry it off to tissues all over the body.

In exchange, the carbon dioxide left over from the oxidation of glucose in the cells passes through the same tissue walls into the alveoli. When the air is exhaled, the carbon dioxide and all the parts of the air that weren't used go back into the atmosphere. Blood leaving the lungs and going to the body is bright red because of the oxygen in it. Blood going back to the lungs, carrying carbon dioxide, is dark red, almost bluish.

There are thousands of alveoli in our lungs, but only people who make an effort to breathe very deeply ever fill most of them. One of the purposes of aerobic (meaning "oxygen using") exercise is to breathe deeply and make the heart work hard. Walking, running, and biking are aerobic exercises. Aerobic exercises strengthen the heart and get the lungs used to taking air more deeply into the alveoli.

Once in the bloodstream, molecules of oxygen are picked up by red blood cells. The main part of these cells is a complex protein molecule called hemoglobin, which contains iron. The oxygen molecules attach themselves to the iron and are transported to the tissue cells, where they detach and do their work of oxidizing sugar. A person with the disease called anemia doesn't have enough iron in the blood to carry all the oxygen the body needs.

Unfortunately, CO (carbon monoxide) binds itself to a hemoglobin molecule even more easily than oxygen does. But the oxygen in CO does not detach from the hemoglobin. Instead, it accumulates, leaving fewer and fewer sites where oxygen can be carried. Because of this a person breathing carbon monoxide soon dies.

A computer model of red blood cells. The hemoglobin in them carries oxygen from the lungs to the body tissues.

Carbon monoxide is odorless, making it one of the most dangerous pollutants in air. It forms when a fuel is not completely burned. It can be given off by a heater that isn't operating properly. Car exhaust always includes some CO. If a running car is closed in a garage, CO can accumulate to dangerous levels. People can be killed by breathing too much CO without knowing that anything is wrong with the air.

Oxygen and the Brain

As oxygen makes its way through the body, fully one-fifth of it—20 percent—is used by the brain. The only time the brain uses less than that is when the rest of the body is very active. Then the muscles require additional oxygen to keep working.

The brain must have a continuous supply of oxygen if it is to continue its work of controlling the body efficiently. If a person is drowning and getting water in the lungs, and is then revived, serious brain damage may have occurred. If the lungs stop sending oxygen to the brain for as little as three or four minutes, a person can afterward have trouble walking, talking, or thinking.

A jet pilot flying at high altitudes must breathe oxygen that has been pressurized, otherwise it will not enter the lungs.

Long before people began to fly, it was known that people who came from low-lying lands had trouble breathing when they climbed to high altitudes. The problem is not only lack of oxygen in the air, it's also lack of air pressure to make the oxygen enter the bloodstream.

A person who does not get enough oxygen suffers a condition called hypoxia. At an altitude of about 3,000 to 3,600 meters (10,000 to 12,000 ft), a climber or pilot might begin to breathe more rapidly. Above that, the ability to think clearly or to make good judgments is affected. By 6,100 meters (20,000 ft), the climber will probably have long since given up or collapsed, and the pilot will have fallen into unconsciousness. Severe or permanent damage done by hypoxia is called anoxia.

Military pilots flying at high altitudes now have a choice of different kinds of oxygen masks. The simplest, used only up to about 6,100 meters (20,000 ft), provides a continuous flow of low-pressure oxygen. The pilot of an airplane going above that altitude generally uses a mask that sends pressurized oxygen into the lungs to make them work.

In passenger planes going to 10,700 to 12,000 meters (35,000 or 40,000 ft), air is pumped into the plane from outside under pressure so that passengers and crew never feel as if they are going higher than about 2,400 meters (8,000 ft). If something happens to the system and the air pressure drops, emergency oxygen masks pop out of the cabinets above the passengers' heads. A passenger must grab a mask and use it immediately.

Fish, In and Out of Water

Fish, lobsters, and various other water-living animals use different processes for getting oxygen out of water than animals who live mostly on land do for getting oxygen out of the atmosphere. There is less O_2 available in water—only about 3 percent, compared with about 21 percent in the atmosphere. In addition, dissolved oxygen does not separate out of water as easily as it does out of the atmosphere.

The gill membrane of a fish is only about 1/25,000 inch thick, but it is folded and refolded many times, giving it a huge area, somewhat like the alveoli of the lungs. The area of a fish's gills may be fifty times larger than the surface area of the whole fish. The gills remove oxygen from the water passing over them, and blood vessels in the gills carry the oxygen to the body.

Anyone with a fish tank knows that fish in a tank with an aerator (a pump that forces air into the water) are more interesting to watch than fish in a tank without an aerator. An aerator adds oxygen to the water. Fish find the oxygen "exhilarating" and they become active. Without enough oxygen, the fish become sluggish. If an aerator fails, the fish owner must stir the water by hand occasionally, until the aerator pump can be fixed. Otherwise the fish will die.

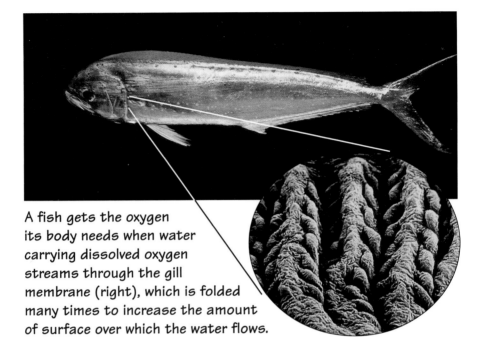

A fish gets the oxygen its body needs when water carrying dissolved oxygen streams through the gill membrane (right), which is folded many times to increase the amount of surface over which the water flows.

Simple animals both on land and in the sea usually exchange gases with the atmosphere or water through their skin. The more complex the animal, the more complex is its respiratory system.

Oxygen usually gets into the ocean water by the churning at the surface. However, oxygen also reaches the living things far, far below the surface, in the deep waters where strange creatures live. It reaches that deep zone through the vertical currents that occur in the Arctic and Antarctic regions.

The bitterly cold surface water—containing oxygen—sinks because it is heavier than the warmer water below it. The sinking water carries oxygen into the depths, where it is used by the living things found there. The cold water is then warmed, which makes it rise again.

Green for Life

Clearly, animals use up a lot of oxygen by converting it to carbon dioxide in respiration. So why don't the living things on Earth use up all the oxygen?

Oxygen is not used up because plants also carry on the opposite process—they make free oxygen out of carbon dioxide. Animals require food from other animals or plants. But green plants can make their own food in the very complicated chemical process known as photosynthesis.

A green chemical called chlorophyll, located in the cells of leaves and certain other plant parts, has the ability to convert carbon dioxide (from air) and water (from soil) into oxygen and sugar in the presence of sunlight. The chlorophyll plays a role in sunlight splitting water into oxygen and hydrogen, which is needed for the process to occur.

In simple form, the following chemical reaction takes place between carbon dioxide and water, in the presence of sunlight:

$$6CO_2 + 6H_2O + sunlight > C_6H_{12}O_6 + 6O_2$$

But there's nothing simple about photosynthesis. Several scientists earned Nobel Prizes for figuring out that there are as many as forty chemical steps involved and describing the complicated reactions in those steps.

This process of sugar-making by plants provides food for both the plants themselves and for all the animals on Earth. If plants had not existed early in Earth's history, animals as we know them would not exist either.

Actually, plants also take in oxygen and give off carbon dioxide. In other words, like animals, they breathe. While the process of photosynthesis goes on only during daylight, respiration goes on both day and night. Both processes slow down in the winter and speed up in the spring.

Most animals depend on the foods produced by plant photosynthesis for their source of energy. But these giant tubeworms live by warm volcanic vents on the ocean floor, where no sunlight reaches. These worms get their energy from eating bacteria that live on chemicals pouring through the vents.

And Then There are the Exceptions

Now you know that all living things require oxygen … but, that isn't always the case. There are certain bacteria called anaerobic (meaning "without air") bacteria that die in the presence of oxygen. Some of them live in our digestive systems, where they break down food into its component chemicals.

Perhaps you've waded in a river and stirred up the bottom so that a horrible odor is released. The odor comes from chemical changes that take place in the muck on the bottom of the river or lake, without the participation of oxygen. Anaerobic bacteria digest the organic material, producing methane (CH_4), which is a foul-smelling gas.

Still other anaerobic living things were not discovered until the 1970s. Robotic measuring devices were dropped to the floor of the Pacific Ocean, where they found springs that spewed out water hot enough to be vapor if it were on the surface. The water, which is heated by contact with molten rock inside the earth, contains huge quantities of minerals, especially sulfur. Against all expectations, the sulfurous environment was found to swarm with bacteria, various marine worms, and even clams— all living without benefit of sunlight and plants. It has been suggested that this is the way life began, long before oxygen-requiring species began to take over the planet.

OZONE— THE GOOD, THE BAD, AND THE RADICAL

There is some ozone, O_3, in the air at all times. But you're most apt to smell it after an electrical storm, when the mighty energy of lightning forces some O_2 molecules apart, and the loose single O atoms quickly link up with other O_2 molecules to become O_3 molecules. Under normal circumstances, the ozone quickly changes back into regular oxygen and the smell goes away.

The very name ozone comes from a Greek word meaning "smell." It was first noticed—and called "electrified air"—in 1785. It was not until 1840 that ozone was discovered and named by a German scientist, Christian Friedrich Schönbein, when he was investigating the smell that

Lightning in the atmosphere temporarily changes some diatomic oxygen (O_2) into triatomic ozone (O_3).

Air brought into a water treatment plant is cleaned, dried, and chilled before it is piped into the ozone generator (the round portion) to be turned into ozone by a lightning-like electrical discharge. The ozone is bubbled through the water to clean it and is then turned back into harmless O_2.

occurred around the electrical equipment he regularly used in his laboratory.

The ability of ozone to turn back into regular oxygen makes it useful in industry as an oxidizer. For example, ozone has a powerful ability to kill microorganisms, making it useful when flushed through sewage to kill bacteria. Many water-treatment plants use ozone. Ozone is so reactive that it must be manufactured where it is to be used.

Ozone for industrial use is manufactured by passing oxygen through a tube with electrical charges running through it. Then the ozone must be used right away, usually as an oxidizer. It can be used to oxidize—and thus neutralize—toxic chemicals. It removes odors from things, also by oxidation, and even disinfects bottled water.

O_3 in the Atmosphere

Ozone in our atmosphere is both good and bad. In the upper atmosphere, where there is no weather, and not even very much oxygen, the sunlight changes O_2 into O_3. The ozone settles in a very thin layer located about 32 kilometers (20 mi) up. This ozone layer has the ability to stop some of the ultraviolet rays from the sun from reaching Earth. Ultraviolet rays, though invisible, are very energetic. They are absorbed by our skin, making us tan or even burn. Ultraviolet rays cause the melanin, or pigment chemical, in our skins, to darken. Some people develop skin cancer from exposure to these ultraviolet rays. Over the centuries, the ozone layer has protected living things from most serious effects of the sun's rays.

Ozone in the lower part of the atmosphere is a different matter. It is one of the main chemicals that pollute our air, making it dangerous to breathe and harmful to plants and animals. It doesn't take much ozone to pollute the atmosphere. Air that has as little as 100 parts ozone per 1 billion parts of air by volume is considered very polluted.

We don't directly put ozone into the air. Its presence is the result of burning fossil fuels such as gasoline and kerosene. When gasoline burns in vehicle engines, for example, the process gives off several compounds of nitrogen and oxygen, referred to as nitrogen oxides and written NO_x. The burning gasoline also gives off various other chemicals called hydrocarbons, molecules containing hydrogen and carbon. When these two types of emissions mix with oxygen in the air in the presence of sunlight, one of the resulting combinations is ozone. Sunny cities with lots of cars usually also have lots of ozone in the air.

Our lungs need oxygen in its O_2 form. The membranes of the nose, throat, and lungs are irritated by O_3. They become sore and congested. People who already have serious lung trouble can die from breathing air polluted by ozone. On hot windless summer days, many city radio and TV stations issue "ozone alerts" that warn people with lung problems to stay indoors.

Plants are also seriously harmed by ozone. In fact, crops rarely thrive in fields located near major highways. It has been

Ozone—The Good, the Bad, and the Radical

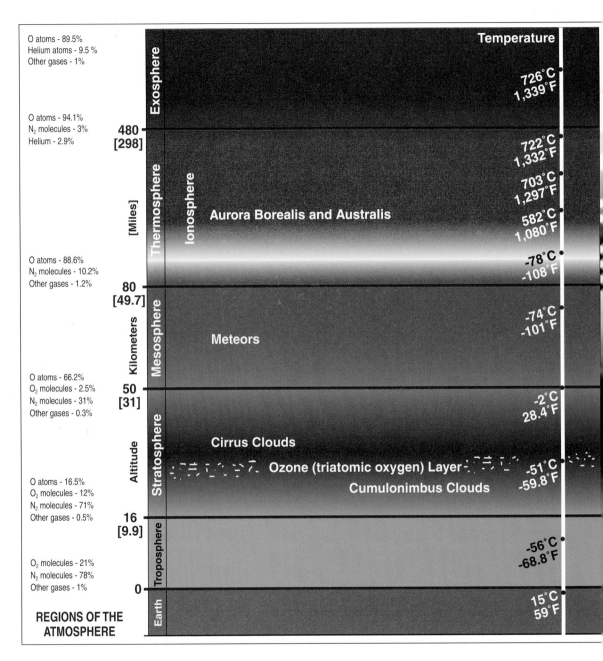

O atoms - 89.5%
Helium atoms - 9.5 %
Other gases - 1%

O atoms - 94.1%
N₂ molecules - 3%
Helium - 2.9%

O atoms - 88.6%
N₂ molecules - 10.2%
Other gases - 1.2%

O atoms - 66.2%
O₂ molecules - 2.5%
N₂ molecules - 31%
Other gases - 0.3%

O atoms - 16.5%
O₂ molecules - 12%
N₂ molecules - 71%
Other gases - 0.5%

O₂ molecules - 21%
N₂ molecules - 78%
Other gases - 1%

REGIONS OF THE ATMOSPHERE

Temperature

726°C
1,339°F

722°C
1,332°F

703°C
1,297°F

582°C
1,080°F

-78°C
-108°F

-74°C
-101°F

-2°C
28.4°F

-51°C
-59.8°F

-56°C
-68.8°F

15°C
59°F

Exosphere

**480
[298]**

Thermosphere

Ionosphere

Aurora Borealis and Australis

**80
[49.7]**

[Miles]

Mesosphere

Kilometers

Meteors

**50
[31]**

Stratosphere

Altitude

Cirrus Clouds

Ozone (triatomic oxygen) Layer

Cumulonimbus Clouds

**16
[9.9]**

Troposphere

0

Earth

estimated that farms could produce 10 percent more food if there were no ozone. In forests located where the wind blows pollution from cities, trees are seriously damaged by ozone. Pine trees are particularly vulnerable because the ozone enters the needles where it interferes with photosynthesis.

Clean Air, Acid Air, and Radicals

Ozone easily combines with water vapor to make hydrogen peroxide (H_2O_2) and hydroxyl radicals (OH). A radical is a partial molecule the atoms of which stay together during a chemical reaction. A hydroxyl radical quickly combines with (oxidizes) other molecules. That's why the OH radical has been called our atmosphere's "vacuum cleaner." It reacts with many unwanted gases, clearing them out of the air we breathe.

CFCs, or chlorofluorocarbons, make up a class of chemicals containing chlorine, fluorine (Fl, element #9), and carbon. CFCs do not react readily with other chemicals. Their unwillingness to react allowed them to be used for many years as industrial cleaners, in spray cans of other chemicals, in making foamy and lightweight plastics, and as the cooling fluid in refrigerators.

Because CFCs don't readily react with other chemicals, the OH radical can't clear them out of the air. Instead, CFCs rises high into the stratosphere, above our weather, to the helpful ozone layer. There, when conditions are right, such as over Antarctica, the ultraviolet portion of sunlight breaks up the CFC molecule. A chlorine atom in the CFCs attaches itself to an ozone atom, breaking it apart. The ozone-layer molecules are gradually disappearing. So, too, is Earth's protection from the sun's harmful ultraviolet rays.

Opposite: A chart showing the percentage of oxygen at various levels of the atmosphere

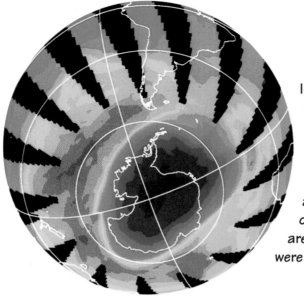

Instruments aboard an Earth Probe satellite regularly measure the "hole" in the ozone layer that forms over the south polar region. Here, the almost black region over Antarctica indicates an almost complete absence of ozone. (The black stripes are areas where measurements were not taken.)

Many countries have outlawed the use of CFCs, but it would take a complete ban on them, as well as a hundred years or more, for these chemicals to stop harming the ozone layer. In the meantime, skin cancer and eye diseases are increasing.

One of the chemicals being substituted for the old CFCs is a chemical identical in all ways except that it has one additional hydrogen atom. This chemical reacts with the OH radical and can be cleaned out of the atmosphere.

Like ozone, the air-cleaning OH radical has its bad side, because it easily makes acids. For example, sulfur dioxide (SO_2), which is given off by burning coal in power plants, combines with the OH radical and makes sulfuric acid:

$$SO_2 + 2OH \rightarrow H_2SO_4$$

The acid can be picked up by the wind and carried long distances. It falls with rain on lakes, forests, and mountainsides, doing damage far from the source of the sulfur.

The hydrogen peroxide made by ozone from water vapor also converts sulfur dioxide to sulfuric acid. These two reactions give the environment a double whammy of the serious pollution called acid rain.

O_2 IN INDUSTRY AND HEALTH

In the past, small amounts of pure oxygen gas were often obtained in a laboratory by heating a compound of potassium (K, element #19). Potassium chlorate ($KClO_3$), which is used in fireworks, combines with manganese dioxide (MnO_2), which is used in making glass and ceramics, and gives off oxygen. Even though the manganese dioxide contains oxygen, that oxygen is not given off. This compound does not participate in the final chemical product. It just speeds the reaction along. Such a nonreacting chemical is called a catalyst.

Industry and the medical profession use much more pure oxygen than can be obtained by such a laboratory process.

Molten pig iron being poured into a special furnace, where more oxygen will be added to make steel

Today, pure oxygen is usually compressed into tanks with steel walls for convenient storage and released through a valve as needed. The liquid oxygen instantly changes into a gas.

Liquid oxygen was first made in 1877 by two chemists working in different places—Louis-Paul Cailletet, a French physicist, and Raoul Pictet, a Swiss chemist. Pictet wanted to learn how to make artificial ice. Cailletet and Pictet discovered that if they lowered the temperature of oxygen, it would turn liquid at –183°C (–297.4°F). The liquid is pale-blue in color. So, too, is the solid "ice" that forms when the temperature is lowered even more, to –218.8°C (–361.8°F).

These days, industrial quantities of liquid oxygen are separated from liquid air. Air is turned into a liquid by compressing it and gradually cooling it to about –198°C (–324.4°F). But liquid air does not become liquid oxygen until the nitrogen and other elements in the air are removed.

You know that when water is heated until it boils (100°C; 212°F), it turns into the gas called water vapor. Liquid air is also "boiled" to separate out its various elements, but the temperature involved is far below zero. The temperature of the liquid air is allowed to rise, and different substances are collected as they turn back into gases at different temperatures. Although helium (the lightest gas after hydrogen) boils off first, it is usually not collected. Nitrogen evaporates back into a gas at about –147°C (–232.6°F) and is collected. Then argon (Ar, element #18) is released. Then, at –183°C (–297.4°F), pure oxygen is collected and immediately compressed back into a liquid again.

This process of separating mixtures of substances by their different boiling points is called fractional distillation. Each part, or fraction, of the substance—in this case, liquid air—is evaporated at a different temperature and then liquefied again. The fractional distillation process also is used to separate gasoline, kerosene, and other substances from petroleum.

Industrial Uses of Oxygen

In the list of top-selling chemicals produced for industrial use, oxygen ranks fourth. It is used in industry in combination with other substances primarily to weld metals together. Pure oxygen is mixed with other gases, such as coal gas, hydrogen, or acetylene, to create a very hot flame that can cut through steel. Acetylene is a flammable gas, C_2H_2, which can be made even hotter by adding oxygen. An oxyacetylene flame can reach more than $3,314°C$ ($6,000°F$). The amount of oxygen used determines just how hot the flame will get.

Oxygen is also a vital part of steel-making. Most iron found in the earth occurs as iron ore, which is a rock of metallic oxides mixed with numerous other impurities. The oxides are reduced in a blast furnace in which oxygen (O_2) is blown through coal,

An oxyacetylene torch being used for welding metal. The addition of oxygen to the acetylene gas makes the flame even hotter.

which is mostly carbon. The result is pig iron, which has taken on about 4.5 percent carbon from the blast. Recycled iron and steel are often added to the pig iron. A little pig iron is used directly for cast-iron and wrought-iron products. Most, however, goes into making steel.

The molten pig iron to be used in making steel is moved to another furnace, where more oxygen is blown into it. This time, much of the carbon content is oxidized to carbon monoxide and carbon dioxide. The resulting product is carbon steel, which contains about 1.3 percent carbon. Various other kinds of steel, having different properties, can be added to the molten mixture for different purposes. When chromium (Cr, element #24) is added, for example, the result is stainless steel, which does not oxidize, or rust, as easily as carbon steel.

Oxygen for Healing

Both compressed and liquid oxygen are also used in large amounts by the medical profession. Anyone with a severe heart or lung problem needs to have oxygen supplies handy to get help in breathing. In a hospital, this used to be done by placing the patient in an oxygen tent. The tent was made by covering a bed with plastic and pumping in oxygen.

Today, most patients get oxygen through a tiny tube placed comfortably into their nostrils. Tents are generally used only for infants and small children who might pull the tube out of their nostrils.

People with medical problems who previously would have had to stay in a hospital for oxygen can now go home with just a small tank of compressed oxygen. They may have to carry a small tank around with them for use at all times, or they may just keep one on hand for emergency use. The tanks for liquid oxygen must be made of steel, but compressed oxygen can be kept in a lighter-weight aluminum tank.

AN OXYGEN CATALOG

Recording Life with Oxides

Iron oxide (Fe_2O_3) is rust, but iron oxide can be useful as well as annoying. Ancient cave people ground iron oxide to a powder to make the red paint they used in pictures painted on cave walls. Many of those paintings have lasted thousands of years.

Modern people have also used iron oxide to record their lives. It has long been the chemical that makes tape recordings possible. Powdered iron oxide, which can be magnetized, is coated on thin plastic tape. As a sound goes through a recording device, an electromagnet moves in response to the sound, adding a pattern of magnetic fields to the particles. The particles behave like tiny magnets. When the tape is played back, those magnetic fields create tiny electric currents that convert to sound.

Chromium dioxide (CrO_2) particles on high-quality recording tape before being rearranged by a magnetic field

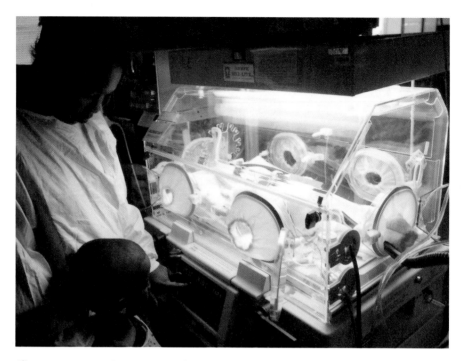

The oxygen environment of a premature infant in an incubator can be measured because of the oxygen's magnetic field.

Magnetic Oxygen

We tend to think of only metals as being magnetic, but liquid oxygen can also be picked up by a magnet. Gaseous oxygen is slightly magnetic, too. The more oxygen there is in an enclosed atmosphere, the more magnetic it is. This fact allows the oxygen content of an enclosed space, such as an infant's incubator, to be calculated by measuring its attraction to a magnet field. By reading the dial on a magnetism detector, nurses in a nursery for premature babies can easily check that their tiny charges are getting the right amount of oxygen, without disturbing them.

Zinc Oxide

When an element combines with oxygen, its characteristics often change completely. Pure zinc (Zn, element #30) is a shiny, slightly bluish metal. But if zinc is combined with oxygen, it becomes zinc oxide—a white powder with a wide range of uses. Zinc oxide (ZnO) is added to rubber to strengthen tires. It serves as a bright white pigment base for paint. And it's used in many cosmetics, including ointments that help dry up acne and that block ultraviolet rays outdoors. It's even used in some photo-copying machines.

Driving with Clay

Oxides of aluminum and silicon are important ingredients in clay, which is used to make ceramics. Ceramics can be as delicate as china plates—so thin you can see light through them—or as sturdy as the tiles on space shuttles that protect astronauts from the great heat of going through the atmosphere.

A truck engine has been made out of ceramic. It has the great advantage over steel because it can develop higher operating temperatures without needing a separate cooling system to cool the engine. A vehicle with a ceramic engine can therefore be much lighter in weight and thus use less fuel. Ceramic engines have not gone into production because of the difficulty of forming their parts. The very thing that makes them so useful—their ability to withstand high temperatures—makes them hard to melt and mold.

In the Exhaust

For many years, cars in the United States have been required to have devices called catalytic converters mounted in the exhaust systems of their engines. Catalytic converters help oxygen in the air oxidize the hydrocarbons from partially burned gasoline, changing them to carbon dioxide and water. In addition, they change harmful carbon monoxide into less harmful carbon dioxide.

This reaction does not happen of its own accord. It requires the presence of the catalyst—the chemical that makes a reaction occur but does not become part of the final product. In a car's catalytic converter, the catalyst is a metallic element such as platinum (Pt, element #78). The reaction of the gases actually takes place on the surface of the metal plate.

When catalytic converters were first required on all cars, the smog levels in cities dropped, but then as the number of cars increased, much of the progress was wiped out. Other ways to reduce automotive pollution are being sought.

The exhaust system of most cars also includes an oxygen sensor that measures the amount of oxygen passing out of the engine in the exhaust gases. If the reading indicates too much or too little oxygen, the fuel-and-air mixture is out of balance, and the engine computer adjusts the air intake of the engine accordingly. Unfortunately, the driver probably won't notice much difference in the smoothness of the ride if the sensor is faulty. But if it doesn't work properly, the engine will use too much fuel, and the gas won't be fully burned, thus adding to pollution.

Following the Atoms

In the past, agricultural scientists have put chemicals such as salts or dyes into water to trace its movement from rain through soil to streams to groundwater. But usually the chemicals were lost along the way and results were not accurate. Now, they have learned that measuring the amount of the isotope oxygen-18, compared to the more abundant O-16, will let them follow a particular volume of water through its path. Every rainstorm, in every location, in every season has a different ratio of O-18 to O-16. This fact allows the scientists to accurately track where

For generations, factories near rivers and lakes have poured their waste into the water. This pollution gradually destroyed the ability of plants and animals to live in the water because the microorganisms that fed on the waste used up all the oxygen in the water.

water came from and where it goes—along with where it picks up pollutants that may be harming our water resources.

Fighting Pollution

Much of the waste that is put into lakes, rivers, or the ocean can be utilized as food by microorganisms, converting it to harmless by-products. For thousands of years, humans have put their own waste into bodies of water with no ill effects, because there was enough oxygen dissolved in the water to support the microorganisms. The amount of oxygen needed for the microorganisms to devour specific waste is called the waste's biological oxygen demand, or BOD.

Throughout history, most bodies of water have cleaned themselves. However, in more recent generations, industrial processes increased the waste in water, and the human population of the planet grew. In many rivers and lakes, there is no longer enough oxygen in the water for the waste to be decomposed. Fish and other water animals have disappeared because the water cannot meet their oxygen requirements. Some parts of rivers and even parts of the ocean are called dead zones. Parts of the Mississippi River and the Gulf of Mexico are dead zones.

Many industrial pollutants contain carbon, hydrogen, nitrogen, sulfur, and phosphorus (P, element #15). The oxygen combines with each of these elements to make carbon dioxide (CO_2), water (H_2O), nitrates (NO_3), phosphates (PO_4), and sulfates (SO_4). Such chemicals also have a BOD, referred to as the biochemical oxygen demand. A product's BOD can be calculated. Book paper, for example, produces chemical waste with a BOD of about 20,000 parts per million parts of water.

The high BOD of paper production explains why so many Wisconsin rivers in the Green Bay-Appleton area, the center of the paper-making industry, were biologically dead for a long time. Only in recent years have paper mills found other ways to dispose of their waste. Once that happened, the work of cleaning the rivers could be started.

Giants Feeding on Oxygen

The Carboniferous Period in Earth's history lasted from 360 million to 280 million years ago. The planet was covered by mighty jungles of ferns and other plants. When they died, the plant matter sank into swamps where there was no oxygen to make them rot. Instead, the plants—under pressure, heat, and time—eventually changed into coal, which is mostly carbon, petroleum, and other forms of hydrocarbons.

Some scientists think the Carboniferous Period could just as appropriately have been called the Oxygeniferous Period because there was such a high concentration of oxygen in the

A museum exhibit shows a gigantic dragonfly in an ancient swamp, when there was more oxygen in the atmosphere than there is today.

atmosphere. All those swampy plants released so much oxygen as the waste product of photosynthesis that the atmosphere's oxygen level might have been as high as 35 percent, compared with today's 21 percent.

Jeffrey Graham of the Scripps Institute of Oceanography in California thinks that the oxygen-rich atmosphere might have supported monster insects. Insects do not have lungs and blood vessels for circulating oxygen. Instead, oxygen in the air has to pass directly through pores in their skin called tracheas. The richer oxygen atmosphere would allow them to grow bigger than they are today. Carboniferous fossils show a dragonfly with a wingspan of 76 centimeters (2.5 ft).

Bleaching

Water, of course, doesn't bleach things, but hydrogen peroxide (H_2O_2)—water with just one oxygen atom added—does.

Hydrogen peroxide is used in permanently coloring hair because it works in three ways on the hair. It softens the central shaft of the hair so that coloring chemicals can go through it. It removes the color from the melanin, the pigment molecules that give color to hair. And it oxidizes the coloring granules that enter the hair cells so they can't be washed out easily.

Stains in fabric can be removed from clothing by allowing the substance that is staining the material to oxidize. Hydrogen peroxide is a useful bleach when very hot water can be used on the fabric. Sodium perborate ($NaBO_3 \cdot 4H_2O$) is also a bleach; it works by changing water into hydrogen peroxide.

Most people today wash clothes in cooler water and so other chemicals must be used to remove stains and dirt. The primary chemical used to bleach laundry at home is sodium hypochlorite ($NaOCl$).

Preventing Oxidation

Antioxidants are chemicals that are added to some materials to prevent them from reacting with oxygen, which might destroy their usefulness. Rubber, for example, can crack when there is a great deal of ozone in the air. An antioxidant added to the rubber formula makes tires last much longer in locations where the air is polluted with ozone.

Look carefully at the ingredients label on a packaged food product from the grocery store and you will probably see the word "preservatives." That usually means that the processed product contains antioxidants to keep the food from spoiling or changing character by oxidation. Fats and oils, for example, become stale, or rancid, by oxidizing, which makes the food taste bad. A chemical called BHA is often used as a preservative. So, too, are vitamin C and vitamin E. Some people take large doses of vitamin E in the hope that it will slow down skin aging, which is an oxidation process.

Resetting Earth's Clock

From the time Earth was formed, its orbit around the sun has varied slightly from time to time, as has the angle at which it tilts in its orbit. When these changes occurred, changes also took place in the planet's climate because of variations in the amount of sunlight striking the surface. Scientists have discovered that the abundance of oxygen isotopes in certain Pacific Ocean microscopic shells has also varied with time. These variations appear to reflect climate changes.

This discovery has allowed scientists to refigure the chronology of Earth's history. Since the early 1960s, they have used a dating technique called potassium-argon dating. Over a predictable period of time, radioactive potassium-40 in a rock sample changes into argon-40 by the acquisition of a proton in its nucleus. The known period is called its half-life. The amount of argon-40 in a sample indicates how old the rock is.

Frequently, the use of oxygen isotopes and the potassium-argon method have given results that varied by as much as 7 percent, and further testing had to be done. However, when the two methods show approximately the same results, scientists have a greater degree of certainty about the timing of major events in our planet's history.

Charting the Path into Space

Most engines must take in oxygen for the fuel to burn. An airplane flying in the lower half of our atmosphere gets plenty of oxygen for combustion from the air. Even at an altitude of almost 15 kilometers (50,000 ft), a jet still gets enough oxygen. But a jet plane cannot fly in the highest levels of the atmosphere because there is not enough oxygen for the engine to work. Only a rocket engine will work there because a rocket carries its own oxygen with it. Liquid oxygen, called LOX, is the most

Robert Goddard, the "Father of Rocketry," in his labora-tory several years after he launched his first rocket

usual source of oxygen for rocket engines.

When Robert Goddard, the "Father of Rocketry," began his experiments in Massachusetts in the 1920s, he became the first person to use liquid oxygen to burn the fuel in a rocket. His first launch, on March 16, 1926, sent his rocket 56 meters (184 ft) high, traveling at 97 kilometers (60 mi) per hour. Today, liquid fueled rockets such as the huge Saturn V have sent heavy manned spacecraft into orbit around the moon.

Rocket engines that use liquid fuel have two tanks—one that carries the actual fuel, such as kerosene or liquid hydrogen, and one that carries the liquid oxygen to make the fuel burn. The two liquids are pumped through pipes into a combustion chamber of the engine, where they are ignited. The action of the exhaust gases exploding out of the nozzles of the engine causes the rocket to go in the opposite direction in reaction. One big advantage of liquid-fuel rockets is that they can be shut off and restarted in space.

Some rockets and missiles are built to use solid fuels in the form of small pellets. Solid fuel is a hard molded rubbery mass containing both the fuel and the oxidizer. The big advantage of solid fuel is that it doesn't require all the heavy tubes, valves, and piping that liquid fuel does. Also, it can be stored for long periods of time in a missile ready to go. However, once combustion is started, the solid fuel continues to burn until it is all used up. Small rockets that carry measuring instruments into the upper atmosphere are often fueled by solid fuel.

"Fire! We've got a fire in the cockpit!"

The National Aeronautics and Space Administration (NASA) was preparing for the first manned flights of the Apollo moon-landing program in the 1960s. It was the task of the Apollo Command Module to keep three astronauts alive during launch, while traveling to and from the moon, and during the fiery re-entry through Earth's atmosphere.

From the beginning, it was planned that the astronauts would breathe pure oxygen at a pressure somewhat higher than the standard air pressure at sea level of 33.87 millibars (14.7 pounds per sq in). The use of normal air would have greatly increased the weight of the module because of all the pipes and valves required. Tests with volunteers showed that humans could live safely for several weeks breathing pure oxygen.

On January 17, 1967, a routine ground test was carried out in preparation for the first manned launch of the Apollo craft. Astronauts Virgil I. "Gus" Grissom, Edward H. White II, and Roger B. Chaffee were participating in a simulated mission—they were to go through all the steps of a real mission but the spacecraft would not actually be launched. Grissom had been a member of the first team of seven Mercury astronauts. White had been the first American to walk in space. Chaffee had not yet made his first flight into space.

The astronauts entered the cramped Command Module, and the hatch was bolted closed. All the various tests of equipment and timing began.

At T minus 10 (ten minutes before the pretend launch and five and a half hours into the complicated test), the voice of Roger Chaffee was heard over the radio saying that there was a fire in the module. The trapped men had no time to say more. A small fire, fed by the oxygen and magnified by the higher air pressure, swept through the chamber, suffocating the men. The fire became so hot so quickly that people on the outside were unable to get close enough to the module to unlock the hatch. The three men became the first American astronauts to lose their lives in a spacecraft.

Investigators decided that a small electrical fire had started in the complex wiring of the module. Even though pure oxygen won't burn by itself, it supports burning once started in something else. So the fire was fed quickly by the pure oxygen atmosphere and by some highly combustible materials.

The Apollo Command Module was redesigned while the program to land humans on the moon was delayed for more than a year. The new version had a hatch that could be opened and exited quickly. Just as important, the atmosphere within the module was changed to a mixture of 40 percent nitrogen and 60 percent oxygen. The astronauts in their suits still breathed pure oxygen, but the atmosphere of mixed gases would keep the module safe before launch. The experts said that in weightlessness after launch, a fire could not spread.

The first flight of the newly designed Command Module took place on October 11, 1968, with astronauts Walter M. Schirra, Walter Cunningham, and Donn F. Eisele aboard. The following July, astronaut Neil Armstrong became the first human to set foot on the moon.

Astronauts flying aboard the Mercury, Gemini, and Apollo

The Apollo Command Module after a deadly oxygen-fed fire killed three astronauts in 1967

spacecraft breathed pure oxygen. The mixture of oxygen and nitrogen used on the Skylab space station allowed the astronauts to live without their spacesuits for several weeks at a time. Astronauts flying in the space shuttle are able to breathe an oxygen-nitrogen mixture or pure oxygen as the requirements of the mission change.

Oxygen in Brief

Name: oxygen, from Greek words meaning "acid-forming"
Symbol: O
Discoverers: Carl Wilhelm Scheele of Sweden, probably about 1772, and, separately, Joseph Priestley of England in 1774
Atomic number: 8
Atomic weight (mass number): 15.9994
Electrons in the shells: 2, 6
Group: 16 (also called 6A); others in group with 6 electrons in second orbital shell include sulfur, selenium, tellurium, and polonium
Period: 2; others in the second period, made up of elements with two electron shells, include lithium, beryllium, boron, carbon, nitrogen, fluorine, and neon
Usual characteristics: a nonmetallic, tasteless, odorless, colorless gas
Density (mass per unit volume): 1.429 grams per liter at 0°C (32°F); only hydrogen, helium, neon, and nitrogen are less dense
Melting point (freezing point): −218.4°C (−362°F)
Boiling point (liquefaction point): −183°C (−297°F)
(Note that both the boiling point and the melting point of ozone are considerably lower.)
Abundance:
      Universe: third most abundant (less than 1%)
      Earth: third most abundant (29.5%)
      Earth's crust: most abundant (49.5%)
      Earth's atmosphere: third most abundant (20.95%)
      Human body: two-thirds by weight
Natural forms: O_2 (common oxygen) and O_3 (ozone)
Stable isotopes (oxygen atoms with a different number of neutrons): O-16 (most common), O-17, O-18
Radioactive isotopes: O-13, O-14, O-15, and O-19 through O-24 are made artificially and are radioactive. They are too low in abundance to be readily observable

Glossary

acid: definitions vary, but basically an acid is a corrosive substance that gives up a positive hydrogen ion, H^+, equal to a proton, when dissolved in water; indicates less than 7 on the pH scale because of its large number of hydrogen ions

alchemy: the combination of science, religion, and magic that preceded chemistry

alkali: a substance, such as a hydroxide or carbonate of an alkali metal, that when dissolved in water causes an increase in the hydroxide ion (OH^-) concentration, thus forming a basic solution.

atom: the smallest amount of an element that exhibits the properties of the element, consisting of protons, electrons, and (usually) neutrons

base: a substance that accepts a hydrogen ion, H^+, when dissolved in water; indicates higher than 7 on the pH scale because of its small number of hydrogen ions

boiling point: the temperature at which a liquid at normal pressure evaporates into a gas, or a solid changes directly (sublimes) into a gas; also, the temperature at which a gas condenses into a liquid or solid

bond: the attractive force linking atoms together in a molecule

catalyst: a substance that causes or speeds a chemical reaction without itself being used up or consumed in the reaction

chemical reaction: a transformation or change in a substance involving the electrons of the chemical elements making up the substance

combustion: burning, or rapid combination of a substance with oxygen, usually producing heat and light

compound: a substance formed by two or more chemical elements bound together by chemical means

covalent bond: a link between two atoms made by the atoms sharing electrons

crystal: a solid substance in which the atoms are arranged in three-dimensional patterns that create smooth outer surfaces, or faces

decompose: to break down a substance into its components

density: the amount of material in a given volume, or space; mass per unit volume; often stated as grams per cubic centimeter (g/cm^3)

diatomic: made up of two atoms

dissolve: to spread evenly throughout the volume of another substance

distillation: the process in which a liquid is heated until it evaporates and the gas is collected and condensed back into a liquid in another container; often used to separate mixtures into their different components

DNA: deoxyribonucleic acid, a chemical in the nucleus of each living cell, which carries genetic information

double bond: the sharing of two pairs of electrons between two atoms in a molecule

electrolysis: the decomposition of a substance by electricity

electrolyte: a substance that when dissolved in water or when liquefied conducts electricity

element: a substance that cannot be split chemically into simpler substances that maintain the same characteristics; each of the 103 naturally occurring chemical elements is made up of atoms of the same kind

evaporate: to change from a liquid to a gas

fossil fuel: petroleum, natural gas, or coal, all of which are formed from the remains of plants and animals

gas: a state of matter in which the atoms or molecules move freely, matching the shape and volume of the container holding it

group: a vertical column in the Periodic Table, with each element having similar physical and chemical characteristics; also called chemical family.

half-life: the period of time required for half of a radioactive element to decay

ion: an atom or molecule that has acquired an electric charge by gaining or losing one or more electrons

ionic bond: a link between two atoms made by one atom taking one or more electrons from the other, giving the two atoms opposite electrical charges, which holds them together

isotope: an atom with a different number of neutrons in its nucleus from other atoms of the same element

mass number: the total of protons and neutrons in the nucleus of an atom

melting point: the temperature at which a solid becomes a liquid, or a liquid changes to a solid

metal: a chemical element that conducts electricity, usually shines, or reflects light, is dense, and can be shaped; about three-quarters of the naturally occurring elements are metals

metalloid: a chemical element that has some characteristics of a metal and some of a nonmetal; includes some elements in groups 13 through 17 in the Periodic Table

molecule: the smallest amount of a substance that has the characteristics of the substance and may consist of one, two or more atoms

neutral: 1) having neither acidic or basic properties; 2) having no electrical charge

neutron: a subatomic particle within the nucleus of all atoms except hydrogen; has no electric charge

nonmetal: a chemical element that does not conduct electricity, is not dense, and is too brittle to be worked; nonmetals easily form ions, and they include some elements in Groups 14 through 17 and all of Group 18 in the Periodic Table

nucleus: 1) the central part of an atom, which has a positive electrical charge from its one or more protons; the nuclei of all atoms except hydrogen also include electrically neutral neutrons; 2) the central portion of most living cells that controls the activities of the cells and contains the genetic material

oxidation: the loss of electrons during a chemical reaction, which occurs in conjunction with reduction; need not necessarily involve the element oxygen

pH: a measure of the acidity of a substance, on a scale of 0 to 14, with 7 being neutral. pH stands for "potential of hydrogen"

photosynthesis: in green plants, the process by which carbon dioxide and water, in the presence of light, are turned into sugars

plastic: any material that can be shaped, especially synthetic substances produced from petroleum

pressure: the force exerted by an object divided by the area over which the force is exerted. The air at sea level exerts a pressure of 1,013 millibars (14.7 pounds per square inch), also called atmospheric pressure

proton: a subatomic particle within the nucleus of all atoms; has a positive electric charge

radical: an atom or molecule that contains an unpaired electron

radioactive: spontaneously emitting high-energy particles

reduction: the gain of electrons, which occurs in conjunction with oxidation

respiration: the process of taking in oxygen and giving off carbon dioxide

shell: a region surrounding the nucleus of an atom in which one or more electrons can occur. The inner shell can hold a maximum of two electrons; others may hold eight or more. If an atom's outer, or valence, shell does not hold its maximum number of electrons, the atom is subject to chemical reactions

solid: a state of matter in which the shape of the collection of atoms or molecules does not depend on the container

solution: a mixture in which one substance is evenly distributed throughout another

sublime: to change directly from a solid to a gas without becoming a liquid first

synthetic: created in a laboratory instead of occurring naturally

triple bond: the sharing of three pairs of electrons between two atoms in a molecule

ultraviolet: electromagnetic radiation which has a wavelength shorter than visible light

valence electron: an electron located in the outer shell of an atom, available to participate in chemical reactions

For Further Information

BOOKS

Atkins, P. W. *The Periodic Kingdom: A Journey into the Land of the Chemical Elements.* NY: Basic Books, 1995

Heiserman, David L. *Exploring Chemical Elements and Their Compounds.* Blue Ridge Summit, PA: Tab Books, 1992

Hoffman, Roald, and Vivian Torrence. *Chemistry Imagined: Reflections on Science.* Washington, DC: Smithsonian Institution Press, 1993

Newton, David E. *Chemical Elements.* Venture Books. Danbury, CT: Franklin Watts, 1994

Yount, Lisa. *Antoine Lavoisier: Founder of Modern Chemistry.* "Great Minds of Science" series. Springfield, NJ: Enslow Publishers, 1997

CD-ROM

Discover the Elements: The Interactive Periodic Table of the Chemical Elements. Paradigm Interactive, Greensboro, NC, 1995

INTERNET SITES

Note that useful sites on the Internet can change and even disappear. If the following site addresses do not work, use a search engine that you find useful, such as Yahoo:

     http://www.yahoo.com

or AltaVista:

     http://altavista.digital.com

A very thorough listing of the major characteristics, uses, and compounds of all the chemical elements can be found at a site called WebElements:

     http://www.shef.ac.uk/~chem/web-elements/

A Canadian site on the Nature of the Environment includes a large section on the elements in the various Earth systems:

     http://www.cent.org/geo12/geo12/htm

Colored photos of various molecules, cells, and biological systems can be viewed at:
http://www.clarityconnect.com/webpages/-cramer/PictureIt/welcome.htm

Many subjects are covered on WWW Virtual Library. It also includes a useful collection of links to other sites:

     http://www.earthsystems.org/Environment/shtml

INDEX